AWAYWARD

BY

JENNIFER KRONOVET

WINNER, 2008 A. POULIN, JR. POETRY PRIZE
SELECTED BY JEAN VALENTINE

Awayward

Poems by
Jennifer Kronovet

Foreword by
Jean Valentine

A. Poulin, Jr. New Poets of America Series, No. 31

BOA Editions, Ltd. ❋ Rochester, NY ❋ 2009

First Edition
09 10 11 12   7 6 5 4 3 2 1

For information about permission to reuse any material from this book
please contact The Permissions Company at www.permissionscompany.com
or e-mail permdude@eclipse.net.

Publications by BOA Editions, Ltd.—a not-for-profit corporation under section
501 (c) (3) of the United States Internal Revenue Code—are made possible with
funds from a variety of sources, including public funds from the New York State
Council on the Arts, a state agency; the Literature Program of the National
Endowment for the Arts; the County of Monroe, NY; the Lannan Foundation
for support of the Lannan Translations Selection Series; the Sonia Raiziss Giop
Charitable Foundation; the Mary S. Mulligan Charitable Trust; the Rochester
Area Community Foundation; the Arts & Cultural Council for Greater Roch-
ester; the Steeple-Jack Fund; the Ames-Amzalak Memorial Trust in memory
of Henry Ames, Semon Amzalak and Dan Amzalak; and contributions from
many individuals nationwide. See Colophon on page 80 for special individual
acknowledgments.

Cover Design: Sandy Knight
Cover Art: "Gray Skies Ahead" by Adam Adach
Interior Design and Composition: Richard Foerster
Manufacturing: BookMobile
BOA Logo: Mirko

Library of Congress Cataloging-in-Publication Data

Kronovet, Jennifer.
  Awayward / Jennifer Kronovet. — 1st ed.
    p. cm. — (New poets of America series ; no. 31
  Winner of the A. Poulin, Jr. Poetry Prize, 2008)
  ISBN 978-1-934414-18-7 (pbk. : alk. paper)
  I. Title.

PS3611.R686A96 2008
811'.6—dc22

                        2008019348

BOA Editions, Ltd.
Nora A. Jones, Executive Director/Publisher
Thom Ward, Editor/Production
Peter Conners, Editor/Marketing
Glenn William, BOA Board Chair
A. Poulin, Jr., Founder (1938–1996)
250 North Goodman Street, Suite 306
Rochester, NY 14607
www.boaeditions.org

NATIONAL
ENDOWMENT
FOR THE ARTS
A great nation
deserves great art.

State of the Arts

NYSCA

II.

III.

❋

FOREWORD

A bold, original lyric voice rises from the very first breath
of this book:

Awayward

A hill is made
less with trees.

A firm thing:
not a look.

We arch. We are
shaped...

The poetry invites you in. When I came across Jennifer
Kronovet's manuscript, I thought of Rilke who says we do not
want to live in an interpreted world. Her poetry does not inter-
pret, but touches the right brain, the part of us that can enjoy
without necessarily understanding, without, as Keats says, "any
irritable reaching after fact and reason." The kind of poetry
that you would not need to paraphrase or defend, but that will
change you.

Another wonderful quality of Kronovet's poetry is that it is
interesting: without having plot, or even a fixed persona, it has
suspense. And complexity, and humor.

Here is one title:

The uniforms. Heh. Waitress, nurse.

Here is a couplet:

A face quickening into faith
that you are still either syrup or golem.

Here is a whole poem:

Night driving

in any city—the boat
of cars, the drift
of ache into motion. The least
physical part of moving: slough.

And. And, I don't know.
Do you know? I don't know.

These poems are full of travel, of exile, of learning, and of
trying to explain. Jennifer Kronovet has returned to New York
City after spending time in Beijing. She seems ideally suited to
write about such experience, and I imagine the experience of
living in Beijing informed her poems. Her openness to syntax is
a delight (and a learning). She writes in "An issue":

Middle of the day,
rain against scrap metal:
the sound removed
of tone—a noon

moving from haze to mud
to a spread of time
not horizontal or not
cultural. Here

rain secrets out mud
from an idea of concrete,
lacing everything
temporary and us,

placeless...

There is great joy in these poems, never forced, but as natural
as their intelligence and courage; and there is sadness, too. For
instance, "I loan you":

Fog hovering above the path
making movielike the site
of let's talk: torn.
We are not. Wrappers
and sky and bottles and body.
Look look look at that.
The money comes back
to me in the form of fruit
I hold softly, I eat sweetly
to try to be to you newly.

And this book has an end. And a depth, and a kind of gal-
lantry. Thank you, Jennifer Kronovet.

—Jean Valentine

❋

FOR ANTHONY

I.

Awayward

A hill is made
less with trees.

A firm thing:
not a look.

We arch. We are
shaped.

A road is made
wider. A look

into the woods
finds abandoned

woods. We are leaving
at the right time

to catch rain
in our movement

toward. Toward.

The Words at First

We guessed: It's you or I.
It's I or it's food or it's forbearance.

It's the kind of word that flip-flops.
It's food and we and

we are riding our bicycles.
It's not getting dark
but it feels like it's getting dark.

And then we live here
and it's windowsill.

PURCHASE

I mime *iron*
and mime *steam*,
miming myself

dissipating in The New World.
The apartment
of different

wiring encodes
the transfer
from her to here.

Here: leaves still cover
the ground—of course
there is season. We can

all agree on falling.
I mime myself agreeing.
I mime brushing

my teeth,
buy tea-flavored
toothpaste.

Disgusting. Yet,
nothing strikes me
as incredibly "foreign."

THE UNIFORMS. HEH. WAITRESS, NURSE.

Wheel as wheel.
Bull as bull.

A kind of clean.
The dirty kind.

A line reaches
from one person to another.

Army-style staff meeting:
You could do better.

Irony? Irony stored
in my stomach like toast.

We pee squatting
with our butts so close

to the ground. Us girls.

Weekend

WE LEFT THE MAIN STREET for the alley. Smoke rose from the meat and it rose from the mouths of men. Here, the men and the women talk through smoke and the men talk to each other through smoke and the women hold hands while they talk. We left a country for this country where I don't make decisions about what I see. I don't allow myself.

In the alley, we slowly decide how to eat and what to say. Does everyone live in a landscape for a reason? On a mountain there must be a reason. In a field, less. In a city, the reason is a tenant. You say the story is the reason. A river is a reason. (We don't have one.) An alley is a reason for eating and avoiding the oncoming car. You make conversation, and I undo it. I'm undoing it.

LOOKY, THE KITES

with blinking lights on the strings.

Groups of men gather.

In between on and off is age and us.

Height is battery-powered and processed

through wind. Wind is processed

through the limbs as weak

and processed by the crowd as owned.

Men gather between age and wind

and one stares at my shirt. My

shift in the wind: my chest

is not the same. It is choral.

This country, if a body, would be

eating potato chips, and enjoying them.

We'd heard they love kites here.

FAITHFULNESS

A whole place changes in a month
like a man marrying a horse.

You don't want to stick your face
into this new intersection

even though it doesn't smell
like rubber anymore:

A face quickening into faith
that you are still either syrup or golem.

I TALK TO ANOTHER MORE THAN MYSELF

The same words: *anathema*,
bibliographic, mark

our language as fallen.
Stencils of trees to decorate trees.

At the museum, you are impressed
by ancient bronze. Metal ribs

of another. I wield a dull knife
to my way of seeing:

the cloud-thoughts, not muscles,
feel the threat. The word-hinges—

like tools of unknown origin—
exposed under the more modern way

to light old artifacts. My use of
you could distill *us*, make room

for another experiment in materials.

AND NOW:

A woman cab driver,
married, drives a stick.
A system decocted
from vantage.

The man fixing the gas leak
is impressed by my lack
of fear. Somewhere a boy
is finishing his report

on the dung beetle.
I repeat forgetting
about cafetoriums
and decals and my eggs.

The man implies he needs
to change everything. I shrug
because I can because
it makes the engine go.

NIGHT DRIVING

in any city—the boat
of cars, the drift
of ache into motion. The least
physical part of moving: slough.

And. And, I don't know.
Do you know? I don't know.

THE FURTHER OUT YOU GO

the harder you are dragged
to your tongue.

There is architecture
and there is your view

of architecture and then
there is the house you can't

leave: Comparison House
brought to you by English.

Less carpeting but more clarifying.
More shelves but less hiding.

Historical as jade and thick as
tomato juice.

You stay where you prefer.
(Until you can't.)

The country from a distance

At dusk the birds roost
in the same two trees: American.
Don't look at me walking
making me that person walking.

We don't meet at the questions. Why
these trees? They stand beside the bakery
that decorates pastries with sugar
made to look like sawdust.

We meet at the corners
of fact: Subway tunnels
present ads appearing to move
but we are moving.

Two children smile closer together
because they are eating bread.

THERE ARE FIVE WAYS TO SAY YOU WANT SOMETHING

One way to avoid attention:
Go. Go. Go. Go. Go.

Excuse me.

The train leaves at what time?
The seats are reserved?
You are a lovely hat?

Cities line up like advertisements for a country.

I have angered you?
You like it here?
Please pass me your wasting time?

Passengers line up to teach me lessons.

In the North, beer can replace rice.
In the middle, beer is made from cucumbers.
In the South, we are all made of sugar.

ALIEN

THEY ARE MADE ALMOST WHOLLY of water which is why they are hard to photograph. They are not hiding from you. I too worry that they can hear my thoughts, but they are all men, I remember, and worry less. Yes, they do love candy. That's true. Like us. When they dream, they sing and hearing it is either disconcerting or shattering. Physical pain always manifests as a color. This may be a language issue. You know, they can't reproduce with us. It would be like trying to mate a fish with a wolf. I am the wolf.

SHOW ME SOMETHING OTHER THAN BRIDGES

The thought-tour ends
at the edge of a row
of houses.

What I want to know most
about the world has never
been hidden:

where am I going
all dressed up
and well-tempered.

When the guides
read her mind
she is as good

as talking. There are
roots and there is dirt
and there are tunnels

so small that water itself
can't force a way down.
I don't need to know

that she hid rocks
to test God
and unburied them

from guilt. Doubt may
be a rock but it is also
a view of sky.

She kissed
her hand once
and it was still her hand.

She lay down
with him in the field
once but it was still

this field. She. She.
And there are others
and she. And I leave

to find a bathroom
knowing I will always
miss the good part.

They Planted

a wall of trees
to protect us
from the desert—

protect the same
thoughts again
and again from leaving.

Clattering forge
of the place-mind:
today today.

Girls cry publicly
to penetrate
the specific.

Community air
creates an event:
his hat!

Leaving is not the word.
We lost leaving last
winter. (*Hid it.*)

Here without the desert-
stance: earth so
flat I'm a person.

THEY HAVE ALWAYS

viewed the night as a wheel
and now I can.

I say *what is day*
and it is a square.

I try to stay awake.
When the wheel of night

rides over us what
marks does it make?

Don't be ridiculous.
We have at last

been proven sentimental:
sleepiness, the night

is a wheel of sound
they tell me. Oh.

THE DAYS SHAPE AROUND OTHERS LIKE A CAST OVER A FAKE INJURY

I miss lettuce.

You say I don't see you but I do.

Light rain.

Once I believed in similarities like luck.

Now, the opposite—I search out difference:

blue, sweetness, sweaters, distance.

An issue

*The Agency of Maintaining Towers sent a memo to the
Institute for Ancient Chronometers: we do not know
under whose jurisdiction the God of Cymbals falls.*

Middle of the day,
rain against scrap metal:
the sound removed
of tone—a noon

moving from haze to mud
to a spread of time
not horizontal or not
cultural. Here

rain secrets out mud
from an idea of concrete,
lacing everything
temporary and us,

placeless. We've lived
in *hush, be still,* but look
at us now, sounding
out each ending.

THE EASIER IT IS TO LIVE HERE

the worse at it I become.

The museum of nature

The earth's humus is made fertile
through the worm's anus.

Horseshoe crabs are experimented upon
for their accessible optic nerve.

I have wanted to be unmoved
by the world. Take the eye apart

and you find that we reverse
things into what we can see:

the stilled vein within the dead ox's face;
your own face in the glass

unchanged by what you might
be thinking: you could survive

in a forest for years if there was a river
and a chance of returning to your life,

or that you would lie down
by the bank and stay until it was

your season, and any thought of return—
a trick as useless as the urge to cup your hands

around the reflection of the sky
and drink from it.

The mountains are made into a road and the land has direction

On one side is the country
and on the other side
is the country, its character
residing in roofs. When I speak
the road I am spilling
the water and dropping my plate.
When I am in the city
and use the language
the city was built within I am
spilling myself into a lake.
Or they who know the language
are twice what I want to say.
And tall. Not wet.
When I arrived I was worse
at speaking but speaking was either
sky or dirt and now the sky
is a different shape and the words,
not symbols, but layers of skin.

APPLES ARE NO LONGER AMERICAN. NOR TRAFFIC.

The gnats swarm
to resemble smoke

ideally—safe
as a breath.

The sawed-off part of change:
the story made up to explain it.

The luck of the fire.
The gnats that saw.

If I forget myself, there
can be chronology: first

I was afraid of smoke,
then resemblance,

then I resembled
something else.

II.

THE INSTITUTE OF CLASSIFICATION AND THE GOVERNMENTAL DEPT. THEREOF

1. I brought the eye

Eye as eye, not *eye*.

The walls were red.
Red is red. Blue is blue.
Color is wall.

A liquid and a solid.

You can see when you are
being stared at.

REPORT: *A problem
unfolds.*

2. I brought the knife collection (inherited)

I was taught:
Blades belong
to striated hills to ice
silvering the branches,
to the overgrowth
of brush. Put a handle
on them: landscape.
The imagined cut
is essential to training,
though painless.
(You can't be entered
if always surface.)
And then imagine
choosing: which
side of the border?
The family? This hill?

Here baby, practice
with this stick.

REPORT: *play.*

3. I brought the lack of nostalgia in the park

The boats won't
because of their
miniature wakes
and the smell
and the accordion.
The children, cheap.
The monument
to the dead man.

We tried this: we are
here until you
find the source—
the small bones like lust
you buried in my fingers.

REPORT: *the stone you moved*
to smooth his seat in the grass.

4. I brought my chest

By which I mean breasts.

They roll their eyes.

REPORT: *Please.* Please body.

5. I brought the sky

the sky that lives
in Redefinition:
liver, standard, teat.

The air—opposite of sea—
thus the sky, the opposite of dead.

The door might close
they say, but they look:
we ignore things until
we can't.

REPORT: *marking today's shame.*

6. I brought prophesy,

told them, no one ever asks me
to define myself in bed. I've learned

to hitchhike myself through process
turning to feeling. Take my cheek.

Bite it. *We* can be evoked through
touch, even *Detroit* can be evoked.

Have you ever been to Detroit?
Thou shalt.

REPORT: *That is disgusting.*

7. I brought our hometowns

A MAN CAN WALK STRAIGHT through his and end up throwing bottles into the river. A man can enter mine and still consider himself a native of aging and sleep. I've thanked him for finding the point equidistant to the centers, but never met him there to pretend that two people meeting by the side of a road is the same as a town.

A town is designed for departures: there are few trash bins and the trees are strict—growing only near houses. Even visitors deserve a tree that looks public, to climb and see what they will be missing.

REPORT: *never going back.*

8. I brought *us*

But I left him at home.

REPORT: *Inconclusive.*

9. I brought wanting to have a baby

The moray, a ferocious eel,
is more formal than the morning
after pill. Everything ignored
can appear to have teeth.

REPORT: *stolen goods.*

10. I brought leaving

And walked in
and out and in
and out.

Departure can
be a stone
in your belly

or a room
in which you made
faces in the mirror.

REPORT (if I had
returned to hear it):

stay.

III.

A SELF-GUIDED TOUR

The "Room for Listening to Rain"
was difficult to locate, but we found it
on the small hill. It wasn't raining
but we heard it, pretended
to hear it, heard its history
as one hears through wood. Wood
that was taken from a shrine
to build a temple, then taken from
the temple to build her house.
We could hear that house—
the sorry/not sorry hum of it.
Under the sound of rain together
because the roof was low and country,
knowing the exact size of not knowing
you. You, through night, then through me.
"She died of illness after all measures
to resuscitate her had been applied."
"She was skilled in German and English."

Her version, with interruptions

Once she stole a boat—*is this how it started*—
at night to bring the pond a gift—
it was a bird of salt—which was taken into its reflection.
But the pond is not the sea. *This is where you lived.*

The lesson of dissolve—*but it was a bird*—sifted
to the bottom of all her actions. *Is this the start
of us?* How she traveled to the sea—*will you*—
is not open for discussion.

She went back for the worst winter—*the worst
winter in years*—and took him—*this is where*—
to see how the pond—*embodied by cold*—ended
in an edge of ice on the sand. She knew it would be foolish

to go out on the ice. *But she did.* And he followed.
They started. They started to see the crack rising
between them. *Meaning nothing*—meaning
something must still be living underneath.

Reinforced concrete

The way you see me was
made palpable to me. There. Boom.

I said *false cognate* which made
me even more probable.

I said that here the word
for *proprietor* is *old board*—

neither affectionate nor cruel.
I ordered food so I could

stop seeing myself saying
myself but the proprietor

misunderstood us as even more
ridiculous than we usually are

so we let him decide everything.
The dishes he served implied

that our use of affection is always
under evaluation. Luckily, you know

to be public even
when no one is watching.

THE ONE OVAL WINDOW

The surface
of this street is sweet
enough to lick.
There is usually
a fee for sacrifice,
ladies, and mine
is a store for rent.
Terrace danger
can not be traded
for river danger
or danger danger.

In this light,
the clouds.

WHERE THE CITY ENDS

stands a type of beauty
we all know how to see.

Still the trees are outlined
in difference.

In Lebanon. In Japan.
We climb for the view.

The tram ride down
turns the day enamel.

Break the crust and we
swarm in gut.

I think, *People know
how to make things*

for comfort. I'm much better
at fear than you. My own trough.

And better at pulse than
admiration: a green structure

in the green trees. If something bad
happens. If it happens here.

SEDIMENT

We met at the bottom of the river.
When you lie, your teeth fill with lead.

Here is a handful of current.
When your teeth are lead, your mouth sinks.

Read it properly: scar tissue.
You repeat yourself: mud mud mud mud.

We met at the bottom of a thought.
When your mouth sinks, floating = the little walk away.

Where do conversations go?
You cannot swallow enough to lower the tide.

RECIPIENT

There was a time when she was less
a concept; each body is less ash
than thought. Away was *away*
like California or Alaska.
Now, never mind.

Feeling harder does earn you
a prize: a new shape named
for you in the world of shapes
where no one lives.

You are more mother, and I
am a partially collapsible line
named Jenny.

TOGETHER

HERE, AT EIGHTEEN ONE MUST CHOOSE to have a bed for dreaming in or a bed for making love in. You think that this would be an easy choice. The sun has set but there is light that makes the country classically itself. If this were before, you would have longed for someone unknown to you. But this person is here, telling you about the first time he realized someone might not like him. She was a nun, and he was a child.

The first years without dreams, you don't know if you've slept. And then you know you have. And then you know you haven't.

One summer you purposefully stay awake together to imagine the forest inhabited by animals drawn by everyone in the country. You choose your words to make it more real, irritated by slips into the easily known. Be specific about how the deer run. How much of it is graceful and how much of it the violent jerk of fear, or of thoughtlessness.

I LOAN YOU

the fee
to touch the border—
palm in the place
of two places feels
the same. Hold your same
foot to the ground
as an anchored raft.
I drift. Countryside
mind games and the stakes
are low: hunger, irritation, lust.

Fog hovering above the path
making movielike the site
of let's talk: torn.
We are not. Wrappers
and sky and bottles and body.
Look look look at that.
The money comes back
to me in the form of fruit
I hold softly, I eat sweetly
to try to be to you newly.

A CONCEPT

At night the air
is densely coal
and breath. I lay down
one breath to be mine
of this. Breathing in unison
with the car heading out.
I lay my head to be glass
and dress and all
arriving thin: the letter
and the shield.

SKY BRIDGE

I name the railing where
I stand like myself *before*:
Hebrew lessons or
tongue on the roof
of my mouth. Or teams.
Each paper thought
attached to the next
with wax to become
by myself or *seeing*
myself stopped
on the bridge. Now,
I am willing to undo
safely, one ligament
at a time—but then,
you're in a funny hat
and we stare
down at the traffic
like animals who never
went to high school.

PREPARE

One could build a ship.
We think. We think
you said ship. You
know I said drive.
You know what I say.

You see me: seeing
the way a highway
has treated a town
as meaningful.
We think it's a town.

You say we are
going, and I know
what you said.
Get ready to make
leaving mean.

FOR US

Hard to know—
always at an end—

the reason for
turning toward yet

another alley of him
while I—in the same

mood—am storing
myself to have

a past, The Past.
What is a lie

for us is holding
the astounding

private. No more
waiting for feeling

to be knowing
like a blade

against the fruit.
Just the feeling

and then saying—
and then another

reason for turning.

Sight; seeing

The town was built because
of a wall and before the wall.

The weather of having said
everything before is making us sing.

Instead of pointing,
we are moving forward. Holding

our little built world
between us as I try

to make a decision in two
languages at once, the decision

becoming a tourist site.
You've seen the pictures.

ATTRACTION

Living is a cow with a plastic side.
See. One stomach gives to the next.
See, nothing's worth hiding.

BEDTIME STORY

THEY NAME IT THE DREAM CITY because it hasn't been built. The park is designed to look like a park. The zoo, a zoo. The museum started planning an exhibition of inkwells to celebrate the one-year anniversary of the museum before the museum was designed. This could be a fiction so wide they built a river to fill it. But it's not. The river was always there. We want the city to be the kind of city the little girl will feel nostalgic about when both happy and depressed. All her colors will be based on the colors of that city. And now the temporary is already seeming permanent: a good sign.

There is a lake and it is the third biggest in the world if we say it is. There have been drownings, accidental, all caused by over-admiration. (Lack of admiration can be equally dangerous.) The police are already stationed in the most beautiful spots to make them a little less lovely and thereby protect us.

I need protecting. I will move into any idea faster than onto a long-awaited city-to-city bus. You like this about me, but I find it a terrible quality in you. After seeing the exhibition of writings by old men in our city you say *let's become old men*. We shut the TV off and you say *let's argue*. About what. *About the Dream City.* And then we decide to put the little things off until the city is finished and we go.

MAKING

Riblike, a case
of one piece—
this is the requested
clutch of us
not coming
to Apology.

Hotel Park next to Pizza
next to Hotel House.
Then a voice bracketing
the movements
drawn inside.

I was a machine
of agitation, heated
and binary and now
I'm sorry.

They dredge up visions

as if fires were always
a town
applied to materials.

There were the fires
that we dressed up
as offerings to belief.

And there were the fires
we made to match
the useless ones.

We manned the thoughts
we couldn't resist
as if they were feelings.

The shallow sun of it:

this week and the next.
You live in a place and
it doesn't know: You fear

the three-wheeled taxi,
a smell too close
to the fruit stand.

The accent is your lemon.
There wasn't a way to mask
myself as real. Instead:

like an egg or a radish.
Alert: pineapple longing or
contact with milk.

I'm going by definition.
And I don't know how to say it.
Just *bye*. Or *bye bye*.

Acknowledgments

I am grateful to the editors of the publications in which the following poems first appeared (sometimes in slightly different forms):

The Brooklyn Rail: "The mountains are made into a road and the land has direction," "Night driving," "The uniforms. Heh. Waitress, nurse.," and "Weekend";

Colorado Review: "Apples are no longer American. Nor traffic.";

Crowd: "Show me something other than bridges";

Fence: "The Institute of Classification and the Governmental Dept. Thereof," "They planted," and "The words at first";

Harp & Altar: "Bedtime story," "For us," and "I talk to another more than myself";

Open City: "Recipient," "A self-guided tour," and "Together";

Ploughshares: "Her version, with interruptions";

A Public Space: "The museum of nature."

Thank you Brett Fletcher Lauer and Stefania Heim for your amazing help, for your friendship, your brains, and for the fun. Thank you Carl Phillips and Mary Jo Bang for your mentorship and your poetry. Thanks to my family, especially Rita, Steven, and Alissa, for your love and support. Thanks to Peter Conners, Thom Ward, Nora Jones, Sandy Knight, and the whole BOA Editions family for your wonderful work. Thanks to many friends for your words, including Kathleen Andersen, Elaine Bleakney,

Jennifer Chang, Gabrielle Giattino, Sarah Mostow, and
Idra Novey. Thank you Anthony Brosnan, my love—I
would go anywhere with you. Thanks most of all to Jean
Valentine.

About the Author

Jennifer Kronovet is the co-founder and co-editor of CIRCUMFERENCE, a journal of poetry in translation. She received an MFA in Poetry from Washington University and an MA in Applied Linguistics from Columbia University Teachers College. Her poems have appeared or are forthcoming in *The Colorado Review*, *Pleiades*, *Ploughshares*, *A Public Space*, and other journals. She has lived in Beijing, Chicago, and St. Louis, and currently lives in New York City, where she was born and raised.

BOA EDITIONS, LTD.
THE A. POULIN, JR. NEW POETS OF AMERICA SERIES

Colophon

Awayward, poems by Jennifer Kronovet, is set in
Linotype Didot, a font based on types cut
by Firman Didot in Paris in 1783; it is
characterized by abrupt changes from thick to
thin strokes and hairline serifs.

The publication of this book is made possible,
in part, by the special support of
the following individuals:

Anonymous

Lawrence Belle　✱　Alan & Nancy Cameros

Bernadette W. Catalana　✱　Gwen & Gary Conners

Barb & Charlie Coté, *in memory of Charlie Coté, Jr. (1987–2005)*

Peter & Suzanne Durant

Pete & Bev French　✱　Robert & Rae Gilson

Judy & Dane Gordon　✱　Kip & Debby Hale

Peter & Robin Hursh　✱　Bob & Willy Hursh

Nora A. Jones

X. J. & Dorothy M. Kennedy　✱　Jack & Gail Langerak

Rosemary & Lewis Lloyd　✱　Irwin Malin

Jim Robie & Edith Matthai

Elissa & Ernie Orlando

Boo Poulin　✱　Paul & Andrea Rubery

Steven O. Russell & Phyllis Rifkin-Russell

Vicki & Richard Schwartz

Midtown Athletic Club / Steven L. Schwartz

The Ship Family, *in honor of Mary M. Stewart*

Sue S. Stewart, *in honor of Stephen L. Raymond*

Pat & Mike Wilder

Glenn & Helen William

✱